Get Smart around:
Your Website Marketing

Darren Hickie

Publisher: DA Properties

Cover Design: Develop and Promote Ltd

© DA Properties (UK) Ltd

ISBN 978-0-9935584-0-5

Contents

<u>Preface</u>

"A common misunderstanding with businesses when they start out, is to get a website first, but this is wrong"

Darren Hickie

I fear that most of us have made this mistake including me in my early days.

This book is meant as a guide to the process of building your website marketing so that it generates leads. It is written with a story of a few long term friends called Luke and Jack.

The 7 step process has been developed over many years by a company I ran. It has produced great results for lots of hungry business owners who are ready to challenge the norm. It is only by implementing and experimenting that you find the most effective process.

Enjoy this book and the others in the series with an open mind.
Darren

Week 1- Introduction to why businesses need a website

Luke crosses the road to the coffee shop; he is meeting his long-term friend Jack for a coffee and a catch up. He is always happy to see Jack, and is in some ways envious of him, but has huge admiration for his success in business. He is looking forward to hearing what he is doing now.

They met through their wives. Their wives were at school together, and they met up again at a party for one of their old school friends. Over the years they both got married and the couples spent lots of time together. Jack and Luke instantly got on well, largely because they had similar interests in business. Jack has set-up, run and sold several businesses over the years. His success has allowed him to keep running some of his businesses by setting them up to run mainly without him. Over the past few months they have not seen each other as often as they used to.

"Hi Luke" said Jack, putting his hand out to shake.

"Hi Jack, great to see you! What do you want to drink?" He asked as he summoned over the waitress.

The waitress comes over with a lovely smile and asks what they would like. Jack gestures to Luke to go first. "I will have a large black coffee please", and Jack orders a peppermint tea.

They spend time catching up with what is going on in each of their lives, and how the children are getting on. Eventually Luke asks "what is going on in your busy business world?"

"I am just in the final stages of appointing a general manager to run one of my businesses, as my previous one left to set-up her own business. I am pleased for her because I feel I helped educate her in my business so she had the confidence to set-up her own."

"Don't you feel annoyed that she is leaving your business, with a hole that needs filling, especially if she was good?" Asked Luke.

"Not really. I feel that at some point everyone needs to move on, and that includes us business owners too. We all sometimes reach a point in a particular business where we just can't take it any further. It is not that they are bad people, or not right for the business, but that they need new challenges to spark their creativity again. A new environment is sometimes a good thing!"

They carried on discussing this for a few minutes, both agreeing that it is not right to carry on working where you are not at your happiest.

The waitress brought their drinks over. Jack uses the distraction as an opportunity to start talking about his own plans. "I was just looking at holidays to America. The family want to go to visit the amusement parks, and we want to explore areas in Florida. We also have a manufacturer there that we have never met, and would like to call in and see them."

"Jack", said Luke, shocked "you have never met your manufacturer?"

"No, but with the change in global communications we have done everything over the internet. We have obviously seen samples, but I would really like to see the manufacturing process. They have also got some new products they think I might be interested in."

"Won't the kids get bored?" asked Luke

"They are very keen to go! When we set up that business they were very much part of it. I am keen for them to learn about business. Even though they have business studies at school, there is a huge difference between the academic and real life!"

"How do you get them to be interested? Mine don't seem to care about what I am doing, they would rather play on their games, or message their friends!"

Jack explains that his do the same, but they are motivated to earn money, and always have roles in the businesses that help them achieve this.

"How will you get the time out of the business to go on this holiday?" Asked Luke.

Jack starts to explain how he has created systems and processes to help the businesses flow on their own, with minimal input from himself. The first part, and one of the most important, is how to get your website working for you, with the way it is set-up and the marketing running from it.

"I have just created 7 essential steps to understand before getting or updating your website, to make it much more effective - for a seminar I have been asked to run for new small businesses" said Jack, "would you like to help me by testing my content?" There is a lot to go through and we are both busy, so can I suggest that we meet up each week over the next 7 weeks? This will also give me time to finish the next section for the following week.

Luke says, "that would be great and give me time to implement what I learn each week and report back."

Luke and Jack continue talking about each other's family and holiday plans before booking the first weekly date in their diaries.

Luke enters Jacks office for the first session and is greeted by his receptionist. She asks him, "is it a large black coffee?" and shows him up to Jacks office.

"Hi Jack" says Luke.

"Hi Luke, how are things?" Says Jack

"Well they are good but I must ask how does your receptionist know I like a large black coffee?" Asks Luke

"Like I said before we have systems in place for running our company and one is to keep a record of someone's favourite drink" answers Jack.

"OK" says Luke "I will have to ask you about that another time, I have to head off in a hour to go networking, shall we see what you can teach me about websites?"

"Yes Luke" says Jack "I will get straight into it. I have tried to keep the presentation simple to understand, for the type of people I am talking to, but there are a lot of very important points to cover.

To most people it seems obvious that you need a website. It seems to be an accepted practice that as soon as you set-up a business you need a website. This in itself is ok for a thought process, but where some businesses get stuck is a lack of planning, or they procrastinate on details that don't matter and don't get it done in a reasonable timescale.

However, although you may feel that the time and effort putting into this is worthwhile, if it's not done properly you'll fail at the first hurdle. Most small business websites, they say around 98%, don't work. This means that only a few websites really work.

The reason behind this is that websites are not very well thought out, or are built by tech people or graphics people with very little, or no understanding of marketing and your business. Some of this responsibility is yours, because when starting out in business most people usually look for the cheapest option. As we all know that is not always best.

If you create a website that looks beautiful but gets nobody to visit it, because it is not ranked in the search engines, or you're not prepared to pay to drive traffic to it, it is a fruitless exercise. You can create a website for a few pounds in a couple of minutes and get it live on the

Internet. There are literally thousands of websites going live every single day.

But on the upside 98% of them are rubbish. So by following this guide you can make sure you're in that 2% that has a website that really works for you.

When I first started my company, I went round the houses trying to get some leads for my business from my website. At that time the Internet was still fairly new and no one really knew how to take advantage of the new medium. I just couldn't get the support I needed from these so called experts, so I took it upon myself to learn the ins and outs of making a website work for a business.

However, what happened, similar to today, is there are numerous websites being produced but never getting found. Unless, of course you manage to send traffic directly via email which was popular back then. It took a few years for other web companies to catch on, but they still have a lack of understanding of how the search engines rank their websites. Some of the web designers today even go around telling you that search engine optimisation doesn't work.

I agree that search engine optimisation has changed over the last few years but it's still important in everything you do, because everyone has a computer.

Think about it for one second, when you go to Google or the other search engines and do some research, you start by typing in keywords. These keywords are what you use to rank your website in the search engines. When you run paid advertising, (if you've had a look into this), you also use keywords. Now, paid advertising will be a lot cheaper if your website is search engine optimised, because the providers want you to be relevant, which means they need to know that the page they are sending the advert to uses the same keyword as the one for the ad. We will cover this in more detail in the paid ads section.

Just think about how people use social media. When you post there is a feature where you can put a # in front of words. A hashtag is the way you mark things for other people to follow, all you do is type a hash and then a word, which is also a keyword. So those people out there saying that search engine optimisation is a waste of time don't really know what they're talking about.

And worse, they are leading you down the wrong path because of their lack of understanding. At the end of the day search engines, websites and social media are all run by computers.

The only way for the computer to know what you're talking about or what you're offering is to index it.

Indexing it means that someone or a computer has read the web page to see what it relates to. Then they store a link to it in their database with some keywords attached so that it can easily be found with those keywords.

There are a lot of different ways in which search engines go about indexing your keywords and the words you use are the main factors, so please bear this in mind when writing copy on your website, adding pictures and posting on social media to drive traffic to your website.

It is not good enough for you just to have a website built now. You need to make sure it has all the elements that are required in this modern world of marketing to make it work and get a return. If you don't get this right you might as well not bother having a website because you are wasting money creating something that no one will ever see, or if they do you will never get to talk to them.

How a website needs to change with business and marketing

One of the reasons websites do not work is that businesses seem to have the idea that once they have built it, they don't need to do anything to it again. This is totally wrong for many reasons.

Your home page is the first page on your website. It is what's called a landing page. Later in the book we will go into the details of what these are, but basically this is the first page that most website visitors start on. You have between 5 and 7 seconds to grab the visitor's attention, to read more and sign post them to more information on your business. Otherwise, they will leave to find someone that has thought about their home page more than you.

This is because we live in a fast paced world where people expect to get the information they are after immediately. There is so much information on the Internet and it loads so quickly that potential customers can afford to skip to the next website if you don't grab their attention within the first few seconds.

To fix this you need to plan your website with the end in mind, which we will call purpose and work back. Knowing your end game and your marketing funnel (which we will learn about later) you can test and measure different words, pictures and text on your home page to get them to the next stage.

All of this will be analysed with numbers and not GUT feeling. (A few years ago one of my coaches told me that I was not to think with my GUT as it stands for Given Up Thinking. Although I totally agree and decisions should be made from the numbers, there is still something to be said for instinct.)

Other things to consider when changing your website;
are seasons. From my many years seeing hundreds of
business owners get better results from their websites I
found that different seasons change the way people
search for things on the internet and the actions they
take. As you will learn later in this book, in the SEO
section, keywords and trends change over time. Not
only do you need to be aware of this, but you also need
to update your website to make best use of it.

As the first page on your website gets most of the
visitors, you also need to keep it fresh. I don't mean
having a total redesign every six months, but the content
and pictures need to be updated on a regular basis. You
need to continue to do this until you get the perfect page
that gets potential customers in and starts a relationship
with them, but bear in mind that people's habits change,
just like fashion trends.

This is much easier to do now, compared to when I
started in early 2000 as it was much more technical. At
that time I was in the corporate world teaching people to
build simple pages on the company's internal website.
The course took three days to show how to create a few
simple pages and add some pictures.

Now you have Content Management Systems (CMS)
like WordPress, Joomla and Magento, they make it easy
to update a website, similar to making changes to a word

processing document. The problem is that most companies that build your website don't give you sufficient training to be able to do this, or you think that it is going to be too hard or technical and don't do it yourself.

Luke, In the following few weeks I am going to convince you why you have to update your website and why you are the best person to do this, plus it is really easy.

 "How was that for an introduction?" asks Jack

Luke says "Well to be honest I was concerned that I would be bored hearing about things I already knew. Now I can see that a website is not just one of those things that everyone just has. It is part of a bigger picture to create a marketing plan, and when done as most people do, it will fail. I am going to have a look at my own site and see what I need to change.

Week 2 – Business marketing purpose

2.1 Only two reasons to have a website

As Luke walks into Jack's office the following week, the receptionist looks up and says "Hi Luke, is it still a large black coffee?"

"Yes please"

"Jack is expecting you, you know your way up, don't you, I will bring the drinks up in a few minutes"

"Hi Jack" said Luke, as he knocked on his office door and walked in.

"How has your week been?" Asks Jack.

Once they have spent a few minutes catching up on their families, Jack asks Luke "Now you have had time to contemplate what we covered last week, do you have any feedback or questions for me?"

"I took a bit of time and had a look at my own website, and I can totally understand what you mean about building a website that looks pretty based on my own personal thoughts rather than building it for a potential customer. I must admit, I have not updated anything on the website for a while as I am just too busy, and I don't have time for all this social media stuff! I had a quick look at our website statistics, and we are getting people visit the website from all over the world, which is not really our customer base. Once people go there they don't stay very long, I think this is called the bounce rate, isn't it? I thought that a high number of visitors was a good sign, but I now understand that they are not really what we are looking to get."

"That's great, thanks for the feedback." Said Jack.

The first thing people miss when building a business website is to understand the purpose.

What does your website do and what is its main reason for being on the web? Is it to sell, information giving or gathering leads? This will then affect the platform you choose, how you word it, lay-it-out and what you include.

There are only two reasons really for having a website these days. In the past it was just acceptable to have a website, because everyone expected you to have one, however this is not necessarily the case in today's fast-moving digital world. The two main reasons we will cover in more detail are:-

- Collect data
- Online shop

Let's cover these in a little more detail and the significance for each one. It's important to get this right from the outset so you know what type of website you are going to create. Don't be tempted to leave it is just as a brochure site because you may as well not bother with the expense or time creating one. You may as well take a chance and create a few entries in some online directories if you just want people to get your phone number. If you are going to take this route, please only use the online business pages as the paper directories are disappearing fast.

Collecting data

There are a variety of ways to set up a website to collect data. These can contain things like calls-to-action, squeeze pages and other forms of entertainment/education that starts a relationship with your visitor on the website, but ultimately grabs their contact details so that, you can continue to build on the relationship with them. Don't worry if you don't know what these are for now.

You will discover in other areas of this training the sorts of things to put on your website and how to create these lead-baits. At this stage I just want to cover the basics of why you need them. Later on you will learn what they are, how to create them and where to use them.

Getting traffic to your website is fairly easy, as we will discover in the later chapters of this book, but once there you need a way to gather the potential customer's details- just like when you are networking you collect business cards.

Note:- I am sure you do something with these cards once you get them! If not, I have a section on this for you later too.

The benefit of a website is that it is open 24/7 and can be scaled up to deal with multiple people at the same time. Unlike when you go networking, you can only have one meaningful conversation at a time. Also the visitors to your website don't all go there looking for the same thing as our personal experiences and backgrounds mean we use different words for the same thing.

To get around this we can create lots of different pages with these different experiences and backgrounds covered. Each of these pages will offer some more information to filter (yes I did say filter for a reason) out the visitors that fit our profile and are ready to spend, from those who are just browsing. This gives you a filter to know who to work on first as a priority compared to those that are still at the browsing stage.

These types of websites are easy to spot because they usually give something away and ask for your address details, or require you to input an email address to download or be sent something.

The whole purpose of these websites is to lead you down a pre-planned path to collect your details, at which point they will start sending you follow-ups to build a relationship with you, by educating you about their product or service.

Really smart business owners take one more step and filter the first contact with you so that they can create segments of interested people. This method allows you to do all your subsequent communications in a much more personalised way. We will cover this in the section about creating and using avatars.

Online shop

This is the most obvious type of website as you basically sell online. You simply list your products and group them in categories and present them to the website visitor.

Unfortunately for you, if you are about to go down this route, there have been hundreds of others launched while you have been thinking about it. It is fairly easy to launch an online shop amongst the millions on the

Internet, so what you need to do is give more information about you and your personality, plus you need to provide more information on each product.

It is very easy to shop online and compare similar products, so you need to do something different to stand out, for example, explain your story or the product story. We will cover stories in more detail later in the book which will help you in all areas of your marketing.

Providing more information on your products could be done with very clever copy writing or videos. Remember that someone buying online needs the product feel and touch described to them as they can't physically touch it. Getting a customer testimonial to go with each product would be a very good thing to do.

Hybrids

If I can I would suggest that an online shop or ecommerce site is also a collecting data one. The reason for this is that most people go to an online shop to buy, as they are a lot further down the sales cycle. So that we maximise our traffic generation activities for those that are not buying now, you should also have data capture forms to build the relationship and cover all bases.

If you shop on Amazon you will see how they master this. When you look at a category you can ask sellers questions (collecting your details and showing interest) and for the next week you will receive emails from Amazon showing products in that category. Give it a go by looking at a category that you would not normally look at and then monitor your emails for the following few days.

In a slightly more advanced approach you can put a tracking code on the visitors' device and send paid adverts just to them for that product. This can be done with Google Ads or Facebook Ads and some other platforms.

Imagine that you have looked at a website for golf clubs but did not buy. You then browse around the internet on sites like online papers or YouTube. Each one of these sites for the next week remind you about golf clubs and might if the marketing company thinks ahead, offer free postage or a discount. Some people will be tempted to go back and buy. Those that don't do anything you can send other adverts to for the next 6 or 12 months.

To do this you MUST put the right code on your website from the beginning or you will be missing out on easy sales. We will look at how and when to do this in your website build.

2.2 Create your marketing funnel first.

What is your avatar?

Stop, don't skip over this chapter because it is crucial to everything you do within your marketing as most web designers don't know about this or can't be bothered, because they usually just want to design or build. Most business owners are not marketers and rely on their web people to do this, but they are not marketers either.

An avatar is a way of profiling an ideal customer you are aiming at. It is a way to identify them as a real person so that you can laser target your marketing material towards them. It means getting to know them, their habits, their likes and interests so that you almost know them as well as your best friend.

The reason that this works so well is that your website pages can be designed and written towards that specific person. This does not mean that you need only aim at one section of your market. You could have several avatars within your business and target markets. But to make things simple, start off with creating one avatar and use it to design your homepage. If you use external people for some of your marketing, like search engine optimisation or social media management, this will also allow them to understand exactly who you are targeting. On top of this it is easy to find exactly where these

customers or potential customers are hanging out so
they can attract them.

Having a comprehensive avatar allows you to bypass all
the wasted money you would have spent on marketing
by trying to advertise to everyone and focus on a smaller
group, allowing you to spend less on your marketing and
get more conversions.

I think one of the reasons why most people skip over
this area is because it takes quite a lot of thought,
understanding and investigation to really narrow down
exactly how you advertise. One of the best ways to do
this, if you've got an existing business, is to pick one or
two of your existing customers and get to know them
very well. Ask them lots of questions which we will
cover in the chart on the next page. You can then find
some common themes of where to get more people just
like them.

When creating an avatar we can start with the basic
information which is;

Gender
Married
Age
Type of lifestyle
Profession
Income

Location

Starting off with these basic bits of information, I would suggest keeping them on a spreadsheet or CRM (customer relationship management) system. This will allow you to browse a group of people together in a very basic form.

You can then use this basic information to have a quick look at how it will work by following the example below.

Working example

Let's say you're selling into the health market. And you're selling products to help people lose weight. Your target market may be women, who are married, aged 40+, live a comfortable lifestyle and work in admin, with £16,000 worth of income, in the Nottingham area.

This then allows us to understand exactly who we are going to market towards. And it also saves a lot of money by not marketing to the wrong places. For example, you wouldn't go and market towards football sites where generally it's mostly men. (Although I do appreciate there are women that are in there 40's that go to football, this market is much smaller). Using this basic information we could go perhaps onto Facebook and target an area of Nottingham, women in particular and then send them to a webpage that we created that has testimonials specifically from other women who are 40+ in the Nottingham area. The women on the webpage would have previously had a weight issue that they have now solved by using your product or service. Further down your webpage you talk about how this product is ideally aimed at women who are 40+, with a busy lifestyle and perhaps work as admin or in an office, and don't get the chance to get out to the gym very often. This webpage will then go on to explain the lifestyle these particular people have and how your products will help them solve the weight issue, with some examples.

You can now see that having the avatar we've created is starting to help, by honing and relating to the exact market that you're working towards. Not only is the avatar then useful for your webpage, but also your social media traffic driving process and any other marketing that you may do. As we talked about back in the search engine optimisation section, this also helps us to clearly define keywords which we will use across our marketing and to optimise our web page to rank higher for that particular market.

I appreciate this is quite generic at this stage and some people may be saying, "my market is not as easy to identify as that." So what you need to do is ask some further questions and dig a bit deeper into the type of person that you're looking for. At this stage most people stop, which is where a lot of people are making a fatal mistake in their marketing by wasting thousands on targeting the wrong people.

These next few questions really explore more thoroughly your understanding of your customer. Some of the examples below may not be appropriate for your particular market and at this point you may decide to stop and decide that the questions are too difficult to answer. If you're happy throwing money away targeting people in a very generic way then that's fine. However, I would beg you to reconsider and continue to delve deeper into this specific profile, remembering that you may create multiple avatars within your business. To start with, really target one because it will make a huge difference to your business and everything you do with your marketing.

So let's have a look at a few more questions that you need to understand about your existing customers and potential ones.

What do they desire, and what are their wants and aspirations?
What problem do they have that you can solve?
Who else is in the market that can solve this problem?
Would they choose them over you, and if so why?
What are their fears, frustrations and challenges?
What keeps them awake at night?
What do they like and dislike?

What do they talk about around the kitchen table?
What books and magazines do they read?
How do they relax? What are their hobbies?
What social media do they use?
What programmes do they watch on TV?
What objections could they have to buying from you?
What are the usual concerns with your line of business?
How do they make their decisions?

This is not an exhaustive list, and you should add and remove questions to suit your own understanding. You are looking to drill down into the groups of people who you want to work with. The smaller the group the easier it is to create a website that works.

By using the set of questions above, you will be able to gain a deeper understanding of who you are marketing towards. From there I usually give them a name so that it's easy for me to remember that I'm marketing towards an individual, they may be called Sarah or Fred for example and from there I can set about designing my webpages making sure the colours reflect those people, that the pictures relate to those people and that I write words that those people understand and use in their everyday life. Spending some time creating these within your business will save you thousands and allow you to bring in customers at a phenomenal rate.

Don't overlook this or skip over this section to race ahead and get your website created before you're ready to put it together. Remember this will drive your colours, your words, your pictures and everything you do around creating your website.

Whichever platform you choose or whatever the purpose of your website, you will want to create a database of relevant leads or people interested in what you have to offer. To do this the "Lead Generation Funnel" on the following page applies, so traffic goes to the right lead-bait on a squeeze page and they enter your nurture sequence that has a trip wire that leads to an offer – your website acts in this capacity as a means of driving traffic into the top of the funnel, so you need to get as many relevant people interested as possible.

Go to the further links page to download a free spreadsheet to track your leads.

Lead generation

What is it?

Lead Generation is the magic key to running a business. It does not matter what business you are in, you will need leads to convert them to customers. It is the constant process of bringing in new customers to buy from you that allows any business to run. If you have this set up correctly you will be able to predict how many and when, you get your new customers. If you have been in business for several years, you will be able to see trends and what marketing you did that brought in the customers at that time.

Leads can be seasonal depending on your business. For example, online retailers have their busiest time around Christmas. If this is the case you need to move into a different phase of lead generation for this time of year.

This might sound like hard work, but it doesn't need to be. I am a big fan of systems, and lead generation can easily be systemised. Once you have a system in place it should be as simple as driving a car. It will need maintenance but if you put fuel in (money or time) it will convert people from not knowing about you or your business to them being a customer.

Lead Generation is about moving people who have never heard of you into being a customer. Starting with your advertising, which creates an enquiry, through to a lead, then to a sales ready lead and a qualified prospect, and finally into a customer. The picture below, illustrates one method very well.

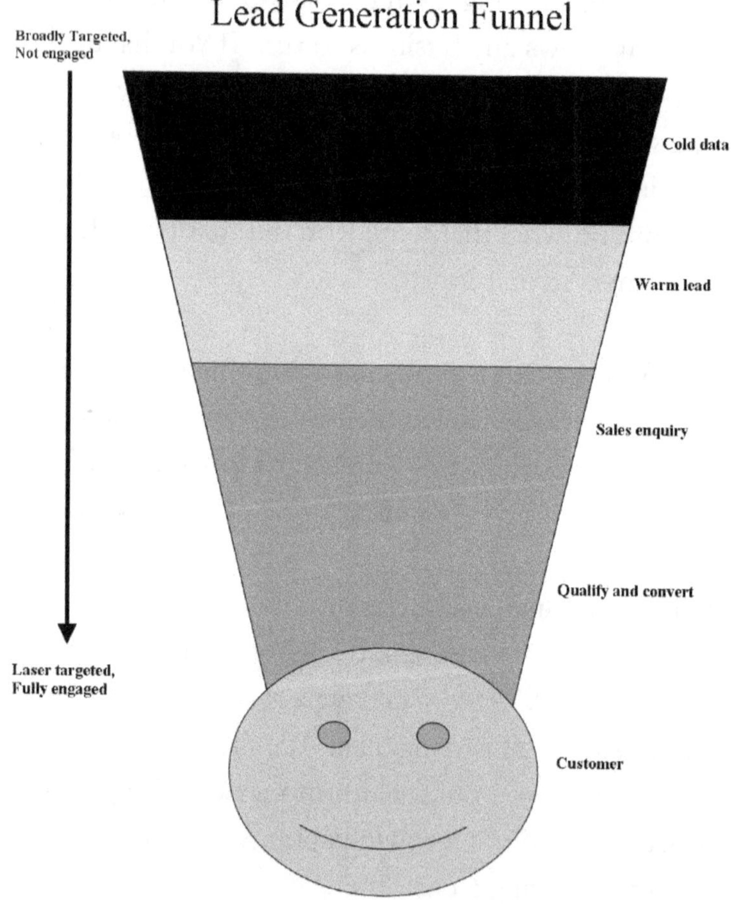

Why is it important?

You probably have a process in your head but have never documented it before. I would suggest creating your own process flow so that you can see who is as what stage, and which steps have the highest drop off.

It does not matter if you work on your own or have a team, you need to work smart. Smart means following a well defined process that is delivered consistently. None of us have massive marketing budgets that we can waste money on, and by having this type of process in your business it will allow you to see which stage is working well and those that are not working so well.

By having such a process in your business helps you plan your sales! What I mean by this, is that, once you have been running your stages for a while you will get a better understanding of how long it takes to convert an advert inquiry into a customer and how many you need to feed into the top to make the sales that you need for this week or month.

By having a well-defined system in place, your business moves from being hard work to plan, to a predictable model. It might sounds boring and hard work but what you are doing at the moment if you are not using this system will make your success much harder to obtain.

How can I implement it?

Start off with a blank sheet of paper (preferably A3) and some post-it notes. I use the little ones as once I get started I find that loads of things get written down.

This first stage needs to be a quick fire round of just putting all your ideas down on paper. If you find that your ideas stop, then simply change where you are sitting, or use a different colour pen.

On each post-it note write all the ways in which you get leads to your business. Once you have exhausted that list, in the bottom right-hand corner of each one write how many leads you have had this year. If you have been reading the dispatch for some time now you will have this on a spreadsheet or your CRM. If not you will need to estimate or look through your bits of paper.

Now put them in order with the highest at the top. I would expect to see at least 12 or more. If not don't worry, as we are going to fix this now. If you are short of ideas for lead generation here is a list to get you started.

Website
Search Engine Optimisation (You are ranked on page one for xxxx keyword)
Facebook

Twitter
LinkedIn
Paid ads on Google
Paid Ads on Facebook
Networking
Direct Mailing
Email marketing
Referrals
Banner re-targeting
Car sign written
Magazine adverts or editorials

If you are suffering from a lack of leads and you only have a few on your list, now is the time to start implementing new ones. Each month I want you to plan and implement a new method of lead generation. This requires you to try a different approach and refine it during the month, so that, you can leave it running, or only need to dip into it once every so often, or even better, get someone else to run it for you. Remember to make sure the costs for running it are taken into account to still achieve profits.

While you get new lead generation processes up and running, please make sure you have follow-up processes in place. We have previously covered this, but basically you need to have steps in place, to call, email and write etc. To keep people moving down the funnel from top to bottom as per the diagram in this chapter.

Around October or November you should be starting to plan your next year. One part of that process will be to look at the customers you gained this year, where they came from and start planning out what you want to achieve next year. Focus on ones that worked well and try to increase them. Those that did not produce the returns you needed should be ditched. Always keep your eyes and ears open for new methods in other industries that are working well and ask yourself, "will this work in mine?"

As always, make sure you have some simple way to store this information, so that, you can report on it. A spreadsheet is a good start, that's what I used to do for the first few years but now I live by my CRM (Customer Relationship Management system). For those new customers that have not come across this yet, just think of it as a way to download all the things you know and do with your customers into one place, that you can search for via an online system.

As a little side note, if you just copy your competitors you will get the same results as them. To get ahead you need to expand your horizon.

"That will do for this week Luke, we have covered quite a lot, but I have a few things for you to go away and do before we meet again next week."

Action points

Create a process flow for your Lead Generation.
Add one new lead generation method per month.

Check your follow up process.

Luke replies "Do you know it's funny, I have heard about this stuff before and was aware of it. I think I do it when I am out face-to-face selling without really thinking about it. It never occurred to me to apply the same principles to a website. There is a lot to take in there, I will take your notes away and feedback to you next week, if that is ok?"

Week 3 - Website layout

Luke arrived the following week looking tired. "You gave me a lot to think about last week, Jack. Obviously my estate agency business is doing ok; I spent all week doing listings and viewings. I realise that we already understand our customer profile, so that makes me feel good. I have been sketching out a rough lead generation funnel; we really need to improve our bounce rate as people leave our site quickly. I think we need a website that collects data, rather than a shop, as people don't actually buy houses online, even though it is usually the first place they look. I have a list of nine lead generation methods to implement over the months to come. Now I just need to understand how to apply this to my website."

"Good", said Jack. The million dollar question is "how should my website be laid out". Unfortunately a lot of websites are based on free templates. Templates may look nice and you have quite a range to choose from, however they're really designed by wannabe or starter designers who want to showcase their work. They are not looking at it from a marketing point of view.

As we discussed before some, of these people are not looking at your market but just looking to put a nice design together. They may have a feeling and understanding over certain colours and certain fancy things that they've seen, or would like to put into their portfolio. It's very kind of them to offer them out free, but with the ever-increasing number of websites and the popularity of cheap easy websites, it's very easy for anyone to pick up one of these free templates.

Templates haven't considered any other marketing elements nor do they have an understanding of your avatar or business, which we've covered in the previous chapter.

Don't go onto the stage of looking at your layout until you fully understand, and have created at least one avatar to build your website layout around.

When someone first lands on your website, they usually start off at your homepage. That is unless you're driving traffic to a specific landing page or squeeze page which we will talk about later on. When landing on your homepage you have around seven seconds to grab their attention, getting them to read more and take action onto the next step. This in itself is a challenge because there's usually so much information to get across.

When considering your layout, in the same way as printed media, the screen has something called 'the fold.' It simply means that the top half of the screen is what grabs their attention, as it is what they see first, and where you have your seven seconds to impress them.

The layout usually depends on your markets and the position you have within your market. For example, if you are selling commoditised products, and you sell lots of something, there is no point trying to position yourself so you look at the top end of your market. This is just not what people expect and within those seven seconds they will be put off by the assumption that this is a high-priced item.

On the opposite side if you have a higher priced item, or work in the top end of the market and your website looks cheap and rubbish, as soon as they land on it they will be turned off.

It has to be very clear which part of the market you're aiming at within your sector, and then needs to look at either conforming to the rules that everybody else works to, or trying to break the mould. Personally I prefer to try something a little different that stands out. Why would you want to be the same as everybody else, because you'll get the same results as everyone else. The idea that you've put time into learning how this all should be structured and set out properly to get those extra leads means you must have thought about being a little bit different from other people in your sector.

Why should they enter your site?

So assuming they have passed the seven second test, they know exactly what you're offering and they want to read a bit more, now you need to give them something that is useful, or direct them to the next stage. The layout of your website should be structured in a way that it breaks down the steps lead will take. This is about also filtering out unsuitable people for your business before moving onto the next step.

The way I like to imagine this, is to break it down into smaller steps and move people from one to the next. At this stage you want to try and capture people's contact details, so that you can begin a relationship with them. The way you go around doing this is offering well-positioned lead bait. Lead bait is usually free information or samples of the products. At this early stage I'd recommend only collecting minimal details, for example name and email address, however, if you have a free product or a book that needs to be posted, obviously you need to collect the full address details also. But additionally collect the email addresses, as you want to do multiple follow-up campaigns that involve both postal responses and emails.

Lead baits have been around in marketing for a long time now. With the increase of postal costs, most people have veered towards the cheaper option of emailing people. However, again I would urge you to consider pushing in an opposite direction. Sending out things in the post is actually quite exciting because, it's not that often you receive something interesting, engaging and tangiable. There is so much electronic information out there it's very easy to dismiss it, forget about it and move on to something else.

From here we need to consider where these lead-baits will appear on the website. There is a lot of research being done around this, looking at where the eye hovers across the screen and where it has the most impact. One of the ones that stood the test of time is the fracture. This is mainly aimed at the Western world but generally is used across most website layouts.

What this means is that if you put an F on the top of your web page layout, you will see that, if you start in the top left-hand corner of the screen most eyes then scan across the top from left to right, then they go back to the left end, scroll halfway down to the end scroll halfway across to the right again, back to the left, then down the page again to the end. This is incredibly powerful when looking at your layout of your website. Unfortunately, as I mentioned several times in this book most web designers and graphic designers are not marketers, and have not spent the time studying the human psychology behind how people use the Internet and their computers.

Implementing the F effect alone will help you take a massive step forward in how your website performs. Once your website is up and running, there is a tool within Google, and some other free tools from other providers, that will allow you to overlay a picture on top of your website to show the hot spots where your visitors put there mouse whilst visiting your website. This will allow you to identify the key areas on your website to see how your layout is working. This is a more complex area of marketing and reporting, using Google Analytics, but is something worth having a look at, at least once or twice a year. Especially if you're considering a new website layout, because you can then inform your designer what works and doesn't work on your old website, rather than relying on their opinion. I'm a huge believer in facts and figures to back up any gut feelings.

Over the years I've tested many types of lead-bait. These range from simple reports to videos, audio downloads and physical books. I find the placing these forms on the right-hand side of the page, with some leading information on the left-hand side of it works the best.

The key to creating your lead-bait is to examine your markets properly using your avatar, and give them something that they will feel is of huge value to them. Simply putting, "sign-up to my newsletter", is a waste of time. Occasionally people may sign-up but there is generally no value perceived in signing up for newsletter, and just the understanding that you will spam them with a load of junk.

3.1 Calls-to-action (CTA)

A CTA is a call-to-action. These are quite simply, ways for your visitors to interact with you on your websites, by means of them taking some action.

You should have at least 3 CTAs above the fold. The fold if you have not heard of it comes from print advertising where the key information needed to come above where the newspaper is folded, so on the top half. This is the same on your website, but the fold relates to where the bottom of the screen is and above. It relates to the first part of your website that you see when you open it.

So you need to have lead-bait, your telephone number and possibly a video as a minimum.

Video is a very popular way to create a call-to-action. In the next section we will look at how to create these. As we know the relationship being built helps people to decide if they want to work with you. A video is a good way to do this, and you need a call-to-action for everyone. Every step of your website marketing is about moving the visitor to the next step.

I have used videos to demo a mobile app and at the end invited the viewer to download the app. This is very effective because it helps them see it in action and allows them very quickly to decide if it is what they might want.

Using videos on other website, like social media ones also helps to drive traffic to your website.

Testimonials are call-to-actions

We're always hearing about the power of testimonials, stories and feedback. I've written about it myself a few times. But sometimes getting customers or clients to give you feedback or leave a review can be difficult. It's not necessarily that their experience wasn't good, it's just that they have other things to do with their time, so they don't get round to it.

One thing you can do is improve your calls-to-action; it could be that you're not asking loudly enough. If you have an e-commerce site, try including a "Leave review" button on each individual product. Make it as easy as possible. If a customer is already logged into your site, don't make them do any more validation in order to leave a review. Include links to places where people can leave reviews, like your social media listings or your entry in a good-quality directory. Put existing reviews and testimonials in strategic places where customers can see them, rather than only using them in the specific place.

The timing plays a big part of it too. When to ask a customer or client for feedback depends on the nature of the product or service they bought from you. It also depends on your 'Unique Selling Point'. If you're trying to broadcast the quality of your customer service, then you'll want to approach the customer or client shortly after they've dealt with you. If, what you want to be known for, is the quality and longevity of what you do, then you'll need to contact them after a much longer period of time to ask how the new shower you fitted is performing, or whatever it is.

Offering incentives for reviews is something that you can do, but you need to be careful of an incentive which is too large, which can be seen as buying positive feedback. Reasonable incentives can include entering everyone who leaves feedback for some kind of competition, or "Please leave a review to receive special offers in the future" – in other words, sign them up for your mailing list! Access to a free download or information sheet when they enter their email address is another one – it's an incentive but not one that's likely to encourage people to be dishonest! Explain that you welcome any feedback or comments, as it helps you to improve your business.

Let's look at "call-to-actions", and how they are important to have on your website, and any other marketing material you produce.

What is a call-to-action?

A call-to-action is something that gets people to do something, or take an action following a prompt from your marketing campaign.

The call-to-action can be anything from clicking a link, through to filling in details to request something from you.

Without calls-to-action your website visitors will go away without doing anything - even if they found something useful on your site. What you need to do is to engage with them and have a way of following up in the future, so that you can build your relationship with them. In my view relationship selling is the most powerful technique around, and more fun compared to cold calling and hard selling.

Calls-to-action can be in any form on your website from a banner, a button, a type of graphic or text that is there to prompt the visitor to click. This would then move them into a sequence of follow-up events, commonly known as a "sales funnel".

The main goal of call-to-actions, is to convert a number of them into 'hot leads' and then finally have a number of new customers from those leads. I have previously written about conversions and your numbers and these are the steps that they come from. I have found from experience that people going into my sales funnel may engage with me for many years before then purchasing from me. Once I have them in my CRM (customer relationship management) system I can start building a relationship with them. I've been practising this method for many years and now have nearly 100,000 people in my leads database, which makes it easy to push an offer based on their segmentation.

Your call-to-action needs to collect some information, usually name and e-mail address and then send them follow-up e-mails. It is best achieved on a landing page and it can be accessed from both your website and social media and any other form of marketing you do. It stretches through to off-line marketing as well, including your leaflets and networking. Even if you've got them in your database already, it is good practice to use a call-to-action to make a sure they are engaged with you and your business.

One of the tricks with a call-to-action is to make sure

that it is of benefit to the person who it is being displayed to; for example if they click on the button, they receive a free gift, discounts/entry to a competition etc.

One of the biggest mistakes that people make is having what they perceive as a call-to-action which says, 'signup to my newsletter'. This infuriates me. It doesn't give any reasons as to why people should bother. Plus most people are bored with newsletters and don't really want to receive them, they already have enough junk in their mailbox. However, if you turn the heading to, download this report in a specific interest area your future customer is looking for, then they would fill in the details and then they will go onto your newsletter system anyway, you are gaining permission to add them at the time of downloading the report.

Ensuring you use active words such as subscribe, register, call or donate means you won't come across as too forceful.

One way to avoid being pushy is to have a time-limited offer or scarcity, by mentioning only a limited number of places available. People are much more motivated to fill it in there and then, rather than considering coming back later, which they don't usually do.

If you're smart with your call-to-actions, you're

guaranteed to gain new leads, which will then lead you towards gaining new customers.

Keeping all this in mind, you also need to think about how many calls-to-action you should have on your site, it is always a good idea to have quite a few, multiple offers, or multiple ways to fill in your call-to-actions, just don't overdo it!

So now you know exactly what a 'call-to-action' is and why it is important, the next step is to make it work!

Initially your call-to-action needs to draw the attention of the visitor, so choosing the sizing and colouring is crucial. There isn't much point in having a good call-to-action if no-one notices it!

Now, I'm not saying you should have it bright yellow and dominating the page; yes it will get it noticed, but definitely not for the right reasons. Try to pick a colour that is in your website's colour scheme, but one that will stand out from the background it is held on. It also needs to be big enough that it can be seen when scanning the page, as sometimes people only scan, but don't read. If the page is not being read thoroughly, the page will be scanned in a Z shape.

This then leads you into the positioning of the call-to-action. Most call-to-action buttons are placed at the top of the page, but there's nothing saying you can't place them anywhere else, just keep in mind how visible and easy they are to spot when a visitor is on your site. Hiding them in amongst text may not work, however placing them in clear eyesight at the bottom of your content, or to the side would work.

Although the appearance of your call-to-action is important, it won't guarantee clicks.

Visitors will not complete a call-to-action just based on appearance, so you need to make sure that you are offering something they really want. They may not want a free report, but they may want a free report guaranteed to boost sales.

Remember to ask yourself the question when adding your call-to-action, "would I complete this action?"

3.2 Videos on your website

Videos on your website are essential and don't need to cost a fortune. They will help to get your message across in a much quicker and engaging way.

Unfortunately most people avoid them because they believe that they are too expensive or difficult to do. This is simply not true. Some of the most successful videos have been recorded on a smart phone and are not the best quality.

Videos you record yourself tend to get across your personality much better than a scripted video that is professionally produced. However there are some key things you need to do so that it does not look tacky.

The types of things that work well in videos are introductions, testimonials and educating people. Be careful using humour in your video as you can quickly put people off. Always keep your personal political views to yourself unless you are using this to repel a certain part of your audience.

When someone visits your website you have around 5 – 7 seconds to grab their attention before they surf to another one. A video at the top of your website that autoplays will get them to stay a bit longer. Once you have their attention you need to convey your message very quickly, in small chunks, to move them from browsing to wanting to read more.

If you don't get your visitors to stay on your website very long, Google and other search engines see this as an indicator that your website is not relevant. On Google Analytics this is recorded as a bounce rate and your organic search engine rankings will drop.

You will have noticed that the word autoplay is mentioned. This is key to grabbing that attention you are after, regardless of your personal likes or dislikes of videos that autoplay.

If you are recording videos on your smart phone you will need to ensure that you have good light behind you, so you might need to move around where you record from. You also need to make sure that you hold the phone or camera as still as possible. There are a number of devices and tripods on the market to do this for smart phones that are not expensive.

Now that you will be recording good pictures you need to test the sound quality. Make sure the environment you record in is quiet and if it is a person you are recording get them to speak louder than a mumble but not shout. They also need to come across as enthusiastic. Do a few test recordings to make sure it sounds right and you are happy with the lighting. Having a few tests will also make the person being recorded feel more comfortable.

If you follow these basic pointers you will get a reasonably good video that you can use on your website. It is better to get a good video on your website than trying to get a perfect video done that never makes it on your site. The next step is to get it on your website.

The best and easiest way to get your video on your website is to use YouTube. It is the second biggest search engine in the world and also owned by Google. It makes it really easy to upload videos and they have a free video editor for any touch ups you might need.

3.3 Headlines

Headlines are very important in any area of your marketing within your business. The headline grabs someone's attention, resonates with what they looking for and encourages them to carry on reading. This applies to both online and off-line marketing.

When it comes to headlines within your website, these are usually key to getting the browsers to stop and read further down your website. This should also be followed by a subheadline which relates to the initial headline and expands on what should have caught their attention in the first place.

Headlines on your websites are also used by search engines to identify whether the keywords within it should be logged and how they should be logged to display your page on the search results.

Creating a compelling headline on the website is an incredibly difficult job because you need to be short and punchy and include keywords to index in the search engines. Places I get some inspiration from, are newspaper headlines. This gets the creative juices flowing. During the process, gather some ideas on how headlines are used to grab attention.

The first headline you'll need to create on your web page is your homepage. Every page linked from that in the structure should have its own headline and subheadline.

Headlines on your website are usually written in a slightly larger text with the sub headline slightly smaller than that. The rest of the text is smaller again, but all the same size. This is achieved by applying some code to your website called CSS. CSS stands for 'cascading style sheets'. This allows you to tag the words on your web page with a standard style that applies a pre-defined set of layout, like font, colour, size, type and other display options.

CSS then allows you to apply a standard across your website to make it easier for visitors to view your site, and it's better on the eye. The way to achieve this is to use a code called H1, this is the headline one and is understood by search engines. Headlines range from H1 to H6, and should be applied consistently across your website. The main headline being H1, the subheading being H2 and so on. If built in this way your website can also be updated and changed very easily by changing one file then apply to all the H1 ones to H6s. It takes a little bit of thought and design from your web people, but it will have enormous benefits for both your search engine rankings and also future updates on your website, plus create a standard within your design.

Considering that you only have a few seconds to catch a browsers attention, when they come across your website, you need to make the headline and subheadline very interesting, so that they grab the visitor's attention and makes them read further. Let's have a look at how we can put together some standard headlines that have been proven to work across the years.

If your page is trying to tell people something specific or get them to do something you might want to consider these suggestions.

- Secret
- New
- How to
- Discount
- A quick way
- Warning
- X Steps to

Depending on what else you are trying to get them to read there are a few types of words that excite visitors and draw them in.

- You

- Your
- Free
- Easy
- Increase
- Why

These are just a few suggestions, to get more ideas just head over to Google and search for "words that can be used in headlines".

Now that you have started creating a few ideas, jot these down on a sheet of paper. At this point just put anything down. When all your ideas have dried up go onto the next step.

Go over the list and create a short list by thinking about what your potential customer will resonate with. Ask yourself what will grab their attention to carry on reading. Make sure that you consider the keywords you also want to include that will rank you higher on the search engines.

Advanced headline note

When creating the perfect headline for your website, a way to test it, if you have the skill, is to run a Google Adwords advert on several of the favourites from the short list. You can test the success of the various headlines by split testing them against one another, keeping the rest of the advert the same just changing the headlines. I would let the adverts run for several hours, or set a budget to spend. The free vouchers that Google send in the post are good for this. Once the experiment has completed you will have a clear winner by looking at the advert that got the most clicks.

3.4 How easy is it to buy from you?

Sounds like a no-brainer, because we all want sales, but one of the big mistakes businesses make is that it simply isn't easy enough to do business with them. It's a competitive world and customers don't need a load of hassle, they'll just go somewhere else.

Forget bells and whistles and publicity stunts, what will make your business a winner at the end of the day is how simple it is for customers to use you for the things they need.

We've all experienced some killer customer service fails, staff who think that customers are there to help them rather than the other way round and deal with enquiries resentfully (and we all know we'd never behave like that!). But this problem is something a lot more subtle, and comes from misunderstanding what goes on in a customer's mind when they're interested in your products or services.

The first thing to think about is how easy it is for customers to find out information about what you do. Do they have to follow a confusing trail of links to find out the information they need? And if they need any extra information before making a decision, do they know where to ask for it without having to go through a long-winded process or entering huge amounts of information? Your own procedures always make sense to you because you're used to them, and probably set them up because they work for you, but potential customers might be finding them a major hurdle and go elsewhere.

When it comes to contacting you, you can't make it too simple or hammer a point home too much, even if it seems obvious, even if you feel like you're repeating yourself. Have the contact details on every page and repeat them again in the copy, and make it clear that there's no obligation when contacting you for information.

Suggesting multiple methods for customers to get in touch, rather than just relying on phone or email for example, makes it more likely that they'll take action. You don't just want to make things easier for customer, but make it comfortable for them as well, and people have different communication channels they feel comfortable with.

Make sure the customers know what you're talking about, by not bombarding them with industry language, and don't make them fill in too much information in order to submit an enquiry. On top of this, reply to all enquiries as quickly as possible, before the customer has a chance to go elsewhere.

One common mistake people make is to have a page on the website which talks about a product, but does not show people how to actually buy it. Having a brochure website is one thing (though it's great if customers can buy online) but we've seen some which neglect to tell customers where they can actually get it.

In the case of an e-commerce site, make sure the shopping cart process is simple and that each product page has a large "buy now" call-to-action button. Make your postal charges and procedures simple and transparent before the customer enters an item into their shopping cart. Nobody wants to be trying to work out a complicated system of postal charges in their head while they're trying to decide whether to buy something. However you're selling, one of the most important things is to make it easy for people to pay, by being properly set-up for multiple payment methods.

I often use what I think of as the 12 year old test for website – is it simple enough that a 12 year old could navigate it easily and take action? This is one way to find out if your procedures are too confusing. Another would be how simple is it for people who didn't grow up with information technology – maybe get your parents to have a look at your website and give you some feedback!

3.5 The power of stories

I recently read an article about a scheme *Oxfam* had been running, and it made me think about the power of stories as a marketing aid. It's something I've had in the back of my mind for a while and the article helped to get my thoughts on the subject together.

Basically, *Oxfam* launched a project called 'Selflife' a few years ago. What happened was that, donated items were given a QR code – the black and white thing which can be read by a mobile phone app – on their tab, which users could then read to find out about the item's past. The new owner of the item could then use the app to update its history.

Oxfam believed that when an item has a story attached to it, it becomes more attractive to customers.

It makes sense. Everyone loves a good story. We're raised on stories almost since birth. They stir emotion and stick in the memory in a way a normal selling point simply won't. This is what's made them a staple of advertising for so long, with many story telling ad campaigns staying in the public consciousness long after they've stopped being run.

In marketing, customer stories are a good way to do this. They take your selling points and put a human face on them, making it easier for the potential customer to relate to and see what you can do for them. A bunch of statistics and notes about performance aren't necessarily going to resonate with people; a story about how your product or service changed someone's life for the better will. Make sure you remember to ask for feedback from your customers, then try integrating case studies and testimonials into your marketing campaigns and see what happens!

Founder stories are good too. Since I've been in business I've noticed that there's an increasing desire from potential customers to know the person behind the organisation. "Meet the team" type pages are becoming a fundamental feature on company websites.

This could be seen as a backlash from the public against dealing with what they see as faceless organisations. They have a desire to go back to basics so they know where they stand. I recently paid a visit to a pub I hadn't been to before which was built up on these lines. It was opened by four men, with the mission statement that they'd sell no food, no spirits, lagers or alcopops, just cask ale. And the customers were pouring in, not just locally, but people who'd come specifically on the train from all around. I wondered if their success was a part of the same phenomenon, the desire to know you're dealing with an expert, with someone who's passionate about what they do and know their stuff.

I recently found myself writing my own founder story for an exciting project we had in the works, and I'll be interested to see how my leads respond to it, and whether it will give them a different perspective on how I can help improve their businesses and lives.

At the moment it's not enough to just read about your products and services and testimonials; people want to hear about you too. If you can make an interesting story out of the founding of your company, whether you built a prototype in your garden shed, had a brainwave on the bus or were spurred to action by a gap in the market, it could be well worth your while to share it. We've found out some interesting stories behind our customers, which they weren't focussing on because they didn't see the relevance. Now it's time to take a second look at your history and see what you can dig up!

"Wow" said Luke, "we have covered a lot today. I did not know about the F effect, I suppose it makes sense that people look at the screen that way. I do agree though, I don't like sites that I have to scroll down to find important details. Call-to-actions are a good thing too, I guess we could give a document away for their details, maybe 'how to sell your house in 21 days?'"

"That's a good idea" Jack replied, "people will always go for something that will help them. Have a think about a story too, and start collecting testimonials from current customers. They will all be powerful for you."

<u>Week 4 – Search Engine Optimisation (SEO)</u>

4.1 What is SEO and why do you need it?

Jack and Luke agree to meet at a restaurant quite close to the airport this week, as Jack is on his way to America for the trip with his family. This restaurant is convenient for both of their schedules.

"Hi Luke, thanks for agreeing to meet me here, I know it is a bit out of your way"

"No problem," said Luke, "it was nice to see your family for a few minutes, we really must have a social get together soon. Anyway, I am loving your input into my website, I feel I am making huge progress. I have created the document on selling your house quickly, for the lead-bait, and I have been playing around with ideas for headlines. I have also looked at other estate agents sites, most of them are like me, and don't do this properly, so once I have it all sorted out, I feel I will have a huge advantage over the competitors."

"Excellent, It is also quite pertinent that we meet here today anyway, as I am going to teach you about SEO. How do you think I found this restaurant? I used a search engine to find it, and the website was at the top of the search box!"

Search Engine Optimisation (SEO) is not just for geeks to play with some black magic to get their website to the top of Google's organic rankings for a short period. It's true that there have been loads of examples of people using black hat methods to fool Google temporarily, but when they get found out, or Google changed the way it ranks their website, they have lost most of the business from not getting the traffic they once did. Those people gambled their luck and it ran out!

When you take a step back and look at everything that you need to do with digital logging and referencing, it is usually carried out with words; keywords. This is how just about everything in the digital world converts binary (the base language of any computer) into something that humans can relate to.

4.2 Keyword research

Why is keyword research so important?

Keyword research is such an important part of SEO as it helps to bring in not just lots of page views, but targeted page views. This is ultimately what you want, as customers who come to your website will be happy with what they find and it will result in more potential sales of your services or products.

What makes a keyword a great keyword?

There are two main aspects to a good keyword that you need to get a balance between to achieve success:

Low competition: You need to find keywords that do not already have such high competition that you wouldn't stand a chance of getting high rankings. Generally people will look mainly on the first page of the search engine, possibly the first few but not often any further. If you are not high up in the rankings, people won't be seeing your site and you won't be getting much traffic.

High number of searches: You need to have keywords that are in high demand with a lot of people searching for them. You won't be bringing in lots of traffic from being high in the rankings for keywords that nobody is searching for.

Long tailed keywords are also very useful; these are phrases rather than just singular words. They make up roughly 70% of searches on the internet so will bring in some good traffic and also generally they are used more by people who know exactly what they want, so are ready to commit to making a purchase, rather than still being at the generally browsing stage.

However, it is very important to keep in mind that all keywords need to be highly relevant. Think about what searches are going to get you results. Don't have keywords just for the fact that they have low competition and high number of searches as this will just result in page views from people who are not part of your target audience, which won't get you any of the results that you are hoping for.

How do I perform effective keyword research?

There are many tools available to research the best keywords available. For example you can use the 'Keyword Planner Tool' in Google AdWords. This is a simple tool which you can type in your URL, some general keywords, and it will give you an extensive list of different possibilities, as well as the number of searches and current competition. This is then available to download as a csv. file so that you can put it into Excel for it to be in a format that you can easily sort through and determine the best keywords for your website.

Once you have got your keywords, you need to make effective use of them and keep checking them regularly.

4.3 Blogging has an effect on SEO

Blogging now is a key element of running your business. It is so important for many reasons including your SEO and getting more visitors to your website. SEO - Search Engine Optimisation is key to getting results from your website, which in turn means we have more visitors, which means you get more enquiries or leads.

Let's have a quick look at how blogging can have an impact on your search engine rankings so that you get higher rankings.

For starters, links are more difficult to get on Google now because of the changes they've made to the way they rank websites. To stop people using spamming links to rank highly, which are irrelevant, Google has put some measures in place to stop this happening such as using the algorithms, *Penguin* and *Panda* etc.

How rankings for keywords are given by Google includes a number of things, the length of stay on your website and also your level of visitors. Another key element is interaction on your website, for example people clicking links or moving around various pages.

One of the things I have commented on a few times is about having the correct keywords. This doesn't mean just picking some words out the air. This means that you need to do some proper research. This takes someone around two hours to do comprehensively.

Over the last two years social media has become a very important factor in getting traffic to your website. This also links into writing blogs and promoting them through social media channels.

Let's go on to having a look at how blogging can improve your website ranking.

First of all you need to be able to write good content or at least be interesting to your audience. If you're not great at this or very comfortable with it, you can always employ someone to do it. However, it is important for you to know the structure of this, to make your copy the most effective for your business.

One of the great things about doing lots of blogging is that you become an expert in your area and of course, everyone knows about your product or service because you are talking about it.

Another good thing about having a blog, is that you can remind people what problems you solve. Remember: when people are searching for your product or service, they're looking for solving problems. For example, if they need more leads they may need to go to a networking event, so you're solving a problem by generating more enquiries.

Blogging also gets feedback from your customers and potential customers.

But blogging takes too much time!

I'm using some software on my iPad called Dragon dictation. This allows me to convert my voice into typed notes to quickly write articles as I come across them. Although I must admit its accuracy isn't brilliant, and it needs a little bit of editing on the PC before it becomes useful. I don't have the problem of writers block because talking through my notes for me, is fairly easy and straightforward.

I can see from the system we have in place that I have 4 to 5 blogs already written, ready to post whenever I need to. It's about staying organised. Start blogging on your websites and publish these to social media to get people coming back. Let people interact with your blog posts. You never know, you might become an expert in your area and generate lots of leads, at the very least you may just have a good record of the things that are going on around you. It's quite scary to start with but once you get going, it becomes quite natural.

As a side note you can easily add some software onto your website that will post a link to your social media channels when a new blog is published.

Blogging tips

There are five top tips that every 'blogger' should know. If you stick to these hints, your website traffic could increase- indefinitely.

Publish your *best* content.

There is a difference between the people you are writing to and yourself. This difference is: You are the expert in the field!

Publishing free content that you could sell, shows knowledge that sets you apart from those who would keep information that could earn revenue a secret. Credibility is gained through this strategy, which can lead to an increase in the traffic to your website! This increases your SEO rankings on search engines. Just make sure to make your content *relevant*!

'Guest blog' and 'guest post' as often as you can.

First, make a list of all the publications you wish to write for. Don't aim small during this process either. It is imperative to choose established and creditable publications to enhance the portfolio you will be working on when doing this!

Then invite popular figures within your industry to prepare small, written pieces you can feature. As they will be in the same field as you, your relevant content will increase significantly. This should have a positive correlating effect on your SEO rankings.

It's <u>not</u> all 'sell, sell, sell'

Harsh sales tactics can often intimidate and scare away

potential and current customers, especially if your blog is irrelevant to their queries and struggles. Dulling down the selling strategies and becoming more client-orientated in your writing will make you a prominent figure for advice. This will significantly increase not only relevance within your website (as you should only be answering questions related to your company/industry) thus increasing website traffic and your SEO rankings.

Write with a personality.

Your writing should have some kind of personality. This doesn't necessarily mean *your* personal humour, dictionary or manner, but you are <u>not</u> aiming for a stifled robotic read. 'Customer Service' is ingrained with your SEO rankings, this means, that when your customers are happy, your SEO rankings, in turn should be making you happy! Just remember: You don't want to put clients off with a stale blog.

Do you write blogs?!

NO! You <u>publish</u>. Respect is key for you to excel in your field- calling your blog a publication will show your business proposals are more professionally orientated. This means your current and prospective clients will; not only have more respect, but more confidence with your advice and expertise.

"I read blogs all the time on my industry" said Luke. "I never even thought of getting them published anywhere, never mind on my website. I will start pulling some of them together so I can add them to it. I will also look at some keywords, as I need to be found above everyone else. Anyway, you had better go, don't want to miss the plane. I will see you in 2 weeks when you get back, that will give me plenty of time to catch up with all the things I want to do with what you are saying."

"See you soon" replied Jack.

Week 5 - Social media

5.1 What's Social media got to do with my website?

Just over two weeks later, Jack and Luke are again
meeting in Jack's office. The receptionist looks up and
offers Luke a black coffee.
"Actually" replied Luke, "would it be alright if I have a
camomile tea today? I am getting my head much clearer
about where I am going, and coffee seems to fog it up
these days!"

"No problem" replied the receptionist, "Pop up to his
office, and I will bring it up"

"Hi Jack, how was America?" Said Luke.

"It was amazing, we met our suppliers, and now have a
few more innovative new products in the pipeline. We
also relaxed and enjoyed the sun and theme parks. How
have you been this last two weeks?" Replied Jack.

Luke told him that he was no longer drinking coffee,
and had followed Jack's lead and moved onto herbal
teas, to keep his head clear. He also told him that he had
added some keywords to his site, and was suddenly
getting hundreds more visitors each week. "It's
incredible, how something so simple can have so much

effect over the number of people who find the pages" said Luke.

Ok, this week we are going to ramp up your social media, by using Facebook, Twitter, and LinkedIn. You should use them all to engage with a wider audience.

I am not going to push you on trying to get your brand out there, because unless you have large budgets like *Coca-Cola* or *Apple* most of us need to focus on getting direct response from our marketing. This is not to say that your company should not have a consistent recognisable look. In most companies this is their logo and the company colours etc.

For this reason you need to make sure that your social media profiles look the same as your website, so that when you send traffic from them to it, they are not confused. I am also not advocating just posting sales messages, there is a fine balance on how you use social media to drive traffic to your website. In fact I have advised customers in some instances where they are very small to only use one social media channel as a website and not spend money on a website. It's all about the right tool for the right job.

We need to cover the basics to find out which channel is best for sending new visitors to your website. We will look at the main ones, but please remember that there are hundreds out there. If you are starting out just choose one and get good at that before adding others. I am sure that you will be too busy once you get your website right to be socialising with people who will never buy from you.

Facebook

Probably the most well-known, Facebook has a very mixed demographic and is very much a social place. Facebook users generally use it to stay in touch with people they already know, and to be entertained. Funny or feel good content goes down well, as do interactive posts – people love it when you're interested in them!

Twitter

Focussed on short, timely messages, Twitter isn't just for sharing what you had for dinner, it's also a place to discuss and debate. While as a business you will probably want to avoid more controversial political discussion, don't be afraid to stick your neck out in other ways and to Tweet multiple times a day.

LinkedIn

Very much a professional network, LinkedIn is good for getting to know people who you can have mutually beneficial relationships with.

Pinterest

A rapidly growing social network, Pinterest is based on re-pinning images to virtual "Pinboards". As a business, you don't have to be on Pinterest to benefit from it; if you install a "pin it" button to your site, visitors can pin your images to their own Pinterest account. This provides a direct link back to your site which people who see the image on Pinterest can follow.

YouTube

The top video sharing site online. YouTube is owned by Google, which is one reason you see a load of YouTube videos in Google searches. Videos are among the most shared content on the Internet, so having a YouTube channel for your business is a good move.

Google+

Google's own social network is a bit of a dark horse at the moment, but it's predicted to be the next big thing in social media. Having a business page there is great for your Google rankings, so it's worth it for that alone. Another good feature of it is that you can divide your contacts into "circles" and share different content with different people

Using social media to promote blogs

When you write a blog post, no matter how good it is, it won't make a difference to your websites traffic unless it is advertised. Where's the best place to do that? Social media!

Blog posts are great ways of adding traffic to your site, and if blogs are written well enough with relevant information, it could give you the chance of gaining new leads and potential clients. The first thing you need to think of is getting it seen.

Each blog post you write should be filled with keywords and great content to increase rankings to search engines.

The most important thing to remember when writing your posts is to make sure that you write to your specific customer audience. This will usually reflect the people who are following you on Twitter or have liked your Facebook page.

Then, once the blog post has been put on your site, you can schedule in some posts on Twitter and Facebook directing people to view the blog with a link to it. The number of people viewing your tweet or Facebook post is higher than the number of people visiting your website, as the followers have constant view of your posts on social media; they won't be constantly looking at your website. Since your followers on these social media platforms will be your customer audience, it is important to think of a catchy and engaging statement on your social media post to get your readers to click onto the blog. Putting something like "Check out our new blog post here!" won't work, choose something that will make people feel the need to click on the link.

If you state why people should look at your latest blog on your social media posting, for example "learn how to...in 3 minutes", you have a higher chance of getting higher levels of referral traffic to your website. Once you have got the reader onto your blog post, you are one step closer to gaining a new lead.

There are no limitations to how many times you can promote a blog post either. Let's say you write 1 blog post per month, you can go on to promote that blog post maybe 2-3 times a week, using a different tag line on each Facebook post or Tweet. This will continuously build the traffic towards your site, while encouraging audience interaction.

It should start to become a routine when you add a new blog to you site; after each blog post has been added, you should promote it on your social media platforms. This, again, is for the simple reason that it's all well and good having a really good blog post, full of relevant content and keywords to improve your SEO, but there won't be an increase in your websites traffic unless people are reading it.

Having a call-to-action on your social media is as important as on your website. If you can get traffic to your site from the call-to-action on your social media, then you're half way there!

In a nutshell, the reason for having a call-to-action on any of your posts is for one reason; creating sales. I'm not saying all your posts should be trying to sell your products, but they need to somehow lead to your website or a contact form for the visitors to land on. There are a few do's and don'ts when making sure your social media has a call-to-action.

If your aim for your post is to get visitors to your site, then link them to the site! It may seem like a simple statement, but there are many occasions where I've clicked on a link that has caught my eye, hoping to be directed to the poster's site, and I've landed elsewhere, or have had to click multiple times before I get to the page I wanted to be on.

Another mistake I have noticed, is one clothing company posted a photo showing new items they had in stock, with the caption being "Take a sneak peek at our spring collection". This seems all well and good, apart from the caption not having any link to where this spring collection may be! If you are trying to guide visitors to a certain area of your site via a post on Facebook or Twitter, make sure there is a link to direct them there!

When writing your posts, think about where you want your audience to go. Whether it's to your homepage, to a specific page on the site, to a download link for a report or app you may want to promote, make sure that you link them to the right page.

Let's say you want to drive some traffic to the blog on your site, it wouldn't be worth adding a link to your post if it takes the visitor straight to your homepage. This would mean they would have to go off and find the blogs themselves, and they may not be willing to do that; if you want someone to visit a specific page, link them to that page! Plus it improves your SEO.

If you have a mobile app for your company, add the link to a landing page, with a description about the app and a download link.

Social media is fast-paced and your posts need links to landing pages.

To improve the links back to your landing pages you need to look over your past posts and see how well you are doing this. Once you have a better understanding of this, you will know where you can add more. If you are having problems fitting in links dues to limits of space on some social media posts, you should use a URL shortener. Just do a search for this in Google, I personally would use the Google one as this will allow you to tag different links in different posts. From that you will have more information in your Google Analytics accounts looking at which ones get how many clicks. If you are going to do this I would suggest that you use different ones for each post so that you can monitor each one.

5.2 Social media segmentation

Still on the theme of social media we will look at the subject of how to split your social media connections to fit with your avatar, by segmenting your connections. One of the things that you might need to find out, is what channel does your avatar use? For example, if you aim at professional services and people over 40 then you should be using LinkedIn and not Twitter.

In today's business marketing you can't really afford to miss out on using social media. There is a lot of information out there telling you which channel to use so I am assuming that you are using the right one for your business. I am going to cover a few different ways to group your connections together so that you can market the right message to the right people.

Facebook lists

Facebook has a built in function to allow you to put different people in different lists. This is very powerful for selecting what messages you send to whom.

As a side note I have been asked several times about having two Facebook accounts. I did at one point but this breaks their terms and conditions. Plus it was very easy to make a mistake and post to the wrong one. It became a massive time drain so I would not recommend doing it.

When you have the right people in the lists you can control who can see your posts. Now you can post personal stuff to Facebook and only show it to friends and family.

Google+ circles

Although not everyone is using this yet, they are up and coming within social media. They have very powerful tools to use for segmenting audiences intuitively. They allow you to share your posts to specific audiences hence the name circles.

Twitter lists

You can create your own Twitter lists or subscribe to others lists. Viewing a list timeline is very helpful. Lists are used for reading tweets only, you can't send to them unless you know how to do it.

To send to a list, you need to format your tweet as normal but at the beginning type @username/listname. The user name is the creator of the list to whom you want to send a tweet. For example you would type @creator/listname, Hi, I am sending this tweet to a list. You can create private lists so that no one knows who is in it. I would do this for competitors so that you can see what they are posting on their timeline. They can block you from following them but you can get around this by having another account.

LinkedIn filtering

LinkedIn offers segmentation based on; target company size, industry, function, seniority and geography. Additionally LinkedIn will tell you how many of your followers match your current filtering options. Free and powerful!

5.3 Keeping score of social media

Social media, like everything else, needs to be measured for effectiveness. There's no point in posting the same things all the time if you don't get interaction from people.

What do you measure for your social media?

Generally things you'd make a note of would be the amount of time you spend on your social media, the number of posts or tweets you make, the number of likes and followers you have, and the number of re-tweets and replies, Facebook comments or shares, amount of referrals to your website from social media sites and the number of leads you get as a result. Another thing to measure on Facebook is the number of people who saw the post, which will be visible to you on your business page as an admin.

With the change in Facebook algorithms, it's becoming harder to get your posts seen by a lot of people without buying paid advertising, but sometimes you'll notice a post has had significantly higher viewing figures than others on your page, which is usually the result of that post having had a lot of interaction. This will have helped spread awareness of your business to people outside your circle of followers.

Going into it in more depth, you can look at what kind of posts get the most interaction, and you may find that people enjoy quotes for example, or videos. This isn't necessarily an invitation to post nothing but quotes or

videos but it can help you think about the tools you use
to market yourself.

Referrals to your website from social media sites can be
measured using your Google Analytics, by looking at the
list of referral sites. It can be useful to view where
exactly on Facebook, Twitter or any other social media
sites the referrals are coming from.

If they mainly come from links you've put in posts, to
blogs for example, it shows that people are finding those
interesting, whereas if more of them are coming from
your profile it suggests that your page is arousing
curiosity and visitors are thinking "Who are these
people? I want to know more."

Marketing via YouTube

Did you know that Google owns YouTube?
This is an ultra-relevant piece of information if you want
to use YouTube for marketing purposes, as it means
exposure on YouTube is linked to exposure on Google.
You've probably noticed that when you do a Google
search you get YouTube video suggestions too.

You don't need expensive professional equipment or
knowledge of filmmaking to create videos, and they can
be a really successful marketing tool.

Although YouTube is owned by Google its algorithm is different and is easier to influence. At the moment, things like multiple keywords, which would get you in trouble with Google, are still a great way to attract YouTube traffic. Here are some tips on increasing your YouTube ranking

1.Only the first 55-60 characters in the title appear in a search match so think about this when you choose your title. Think of it as a mini billboard for your video. The title needs to use plenty of keywords – as many as possible but in a way that makes sense.

2.You get 5,000 characters to use in the video description. Use as many of them as possible and stuff them with keywords. Try and use all your keywords in the description but don't repeat them in a way that looks spamming. Be sensible.

3.You can use as many keywords as you like in the video tags. Use quotes around the phrases you want to rank highly for.

4.Youtube now has a "time watched" factor, which means you get rewarded not just for clicks but for how long users stay on YouTube after finishing your video, browsing recommended videos etc.

5.As with normal SEO, incoming links are important.

Each YouTube video has its own unique URL, and this is what you need to get links to.

You don't even necessarily need a full website to market on YouTube; a squeeze page for people to visit and opt-in to for your mailing list will do.

I hope this has given you a bit of assistance in what will be best for you. What do you use at the moment?

Luke says, "I have a personal Facebook page, and the company has dabbled with Twitter, but you have motivated me again to do it differently! I am going to create a business page on Facebook for the agency, and regularly blog to this and twitter, as well as advertise houses, and use my lead-bait to get more customers!"

"Great" said Jack, "Lets reconvene the same time next week. I am looking forward to seeing your social media, send me the links when you have created them, and I will share them with my network too. I have faith in what you are doing."

Week 6 - Squeeze Page & Landing Page

6.1 What is a squeeze page?

"Hi Jack", said Luke when they met the next week. "I think I am finally getting the hang of this website marketing, the email addresses are coming in thick and fast, we are getting more people selling their houses through us, and I have actually had one of my blogs published in an industry magazine! I'm sorry to come in and ramble on like this, but I am so excited that it is all working."

"No problem", Jack replied, I am glad it is going well. Now I am going to explain how to know where your leads come from, by using a squeeze page.

A squeeze page is simply a page on your website that only allows the visitor to give you information. On that page you do not have a menu or links to other pages. You only have a form for squeezing information out of someone. These pages have been used a lot and visitors are aware of what you are doing.

You do need to be careful with these pages as the paid ads sites don't like you sending traffic to them as it does not enhance the user experience. You also need to be careful of the information you put on these pages because you need to keep the visitor on the page for over 30 seconds to make sure you don't get marked down for a high bounce rate on your site. Your bounce rate is the measure of someone leaving your website in a very short period, for example, less than 30 seconds.

A squeeze page is very good for building your database at the beginning of your marketing funnel. Because they have been used a lot over the last few years you need to make the offer very compelling to gather details, but get this right and you will have a huge engaged and qualified database to work with.

Many times I get asked the question:

'What is the difference between a squeeze page and a landing page; aren't they essentially the same thing?'

Well the short answer is no, they aren't! In fact both pages have very different functions and act in specific ways on your site.

Defining a squeeze page

The definition of a squeeze page is, a simplified landing page, with the very specific function of encouraging the visitor to perform a task or action. The most common action to be taken on a squeeze page is to try and get the visitor to enter their contact details and email address in exchange for something valuable you can offer them. It's called a squeeze page because you are in essence squeezing the contact details out of your potential customer. The offer you make to them in exchange for their details is a lead-bait and is usually something like an e-book, fact sheet or video series. The point being it is something of use that the customer desires without having to pay for. It lures them in!

Why are 'squeeze pages' so important to your marketing?

Squeeze pages are extremely important within all areas of digital marketing because they extract potential customer's details and allow you to enter into a conversation with them. Once you have their valuable email address you can begin to build up a relationship with offers, content giveaways, testimonials, e-mail marketing and so forth.

A squeeze page massively increases the chances you'll get hold of the visitor's contact details, as there is little else for them to do on this type of page. A landing page, on the otherhand, will typically have a multitude of areas to read, explore and click on whereas a squeeze page is simply there to capture contact details. There is no other function to it.

Here is an example of a really good squeeze page to give you some comparison:

How to set up a Google Analytics web tracking code on your 'squeeze page'

When driving traffic to your squeeze page you may want to utilise a tracking service such as Google Analytics to monitor your page's effectiveness.

You can do this yourself by creating a Google Analytics account and grabbing the code snippet to place on the HTML of your squeeze page. However, if this sounds a bit too complicated then get your web developer to help.

You could also try setting up custom audiences in Facebook in order to remarket from your squeeze page. Remarketing allows Facebook to identify the type of customer that you are referring to your squeeze page, so that you can then target your advertisements specifically at people who have visited your page at some stage. Again, the process of tracking this can prove to be a bit tricky so if you do need any help ask your developer.

6.2 Landing page

Defining a landing page

Let's begin by exploring what the differences are, starting off with the landing page.

The definition of a landing page is:

'A web page that someone lands on when they click on a link from somewhere other than your site'.

The link could be placed on anything really, from an email to an advert on social media. But what a landing page does do, is direct your potential customer to a very specific part of your site.

Landing pages don't necessarily have to be about the hard sell, in fact it's best if they're not. Instead a landing page should be all about offering the visitor highly relevant and useful information about your product or service.

Here is just one of many examples of a landing page layout:

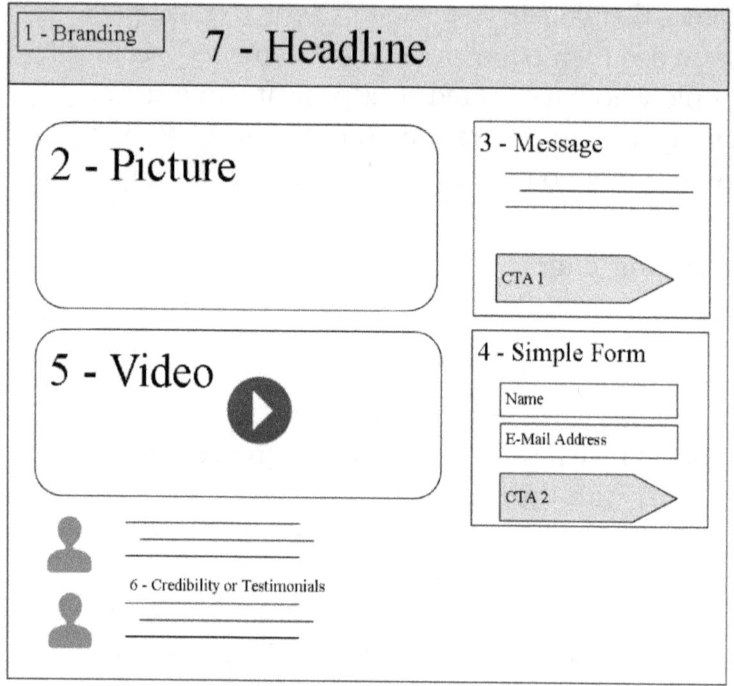

1 = Brand/Logo
2 = Picture
3 = Message
4 = CTA Form
5 = Video Message
6 = Testimonials
7 = Headline

Include a logo, status indicator, headline, image of the lead-bait or video, opt-in button, social proof statement, sub-heading, and three bullet points. At the end add another opt-in button, as this saves the user having to go back up once they have read the full page. You could also use words like 'You will receive the lead-bait immediately after entering your email above'

Landling pages can also be combined with lead-baits (sometimes called lead-magnets) to collect contact details. Below is an example of what I have found works as a layout.

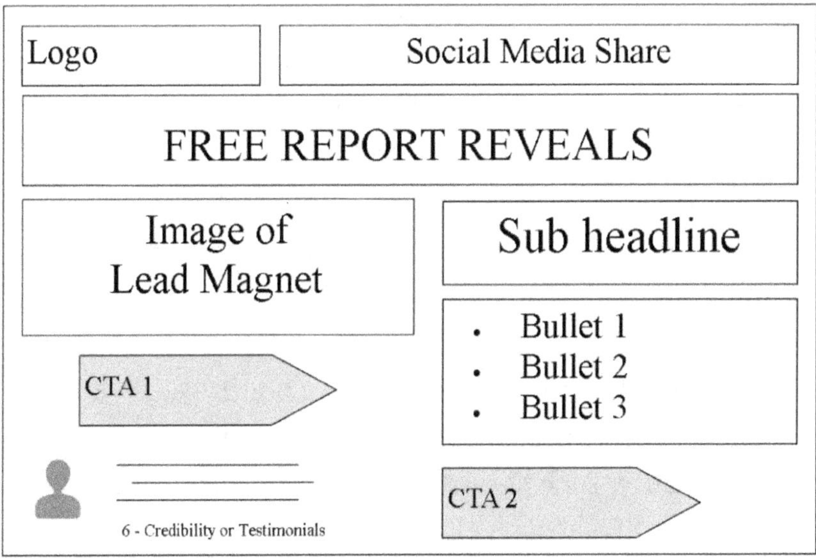

CTA buttons work well in yellow, orange and green.

Most of your website should be made up of landing pages to firstly inform your visitor that they are in the right place, then spark their interest and finally finish with a call-to-action. This simple process is very effective in filling your marketing funnel.

There is no one right way to build a perfect page that can be applied to everyone. You need to start with some tried and tested layouts and then test different layouts with split-testing.

6.3 Split testing

Once you have your marketing up and running the next stage is to improve it. The best way to go about this is to make small changes and measure the results. This is carried out by using the measurements before all the changes were made and after the changes were made, as a comparison to see which one is better. This is commonly known as split testing and sometimes referred to as A/B testing.

It is a logical method of carrying out controlled experiments with a simple goal of improving website performance, such as clicks, form completions and purchases. To ensure a fair comparison, it is best to compare two different samples at exactly the same time to avoid conflict on the times at which the test was conducted.

The type of changes that you may consider in split-testing should be systematic changes like the text on a headline or descriptions of products, small layout changes and sizes or colours of buttons.

Run these changes over a few days and when you make these small increments in performance the overall compound effect will be massive.

There are various programs to do this, for example *optimisely.com* or you can simply tell Google Analytics to split test and to distribute the traffic equally across two versions of the same page with the minor differences. Obviously you can apply this to your paid advertising as well as making sure that everything at that point where the pages changed is exactly the same, otherwise you will skew the results.

Split-testing on a regular basis is a must to improve the performance of your website and to get the most out of your investment. This is a particularly important factor if you are using squeeze pages or landing pages. Once you have the process set-up and refined, the return on investment will create an asset for the business that you can use many times over.

When split testing try using the simple matrix below to monitor your improvements using Google Analytics.

	Base page	Headline to now	CTA button to Green	CTA button to Orange	Bigger picture
Measure	1 Oct	5 Oct	8 Oct	15 Oct	21 Oct
Traffic	100	111	110	112	114
Filled in form	10	13	14	17	21
Conversion %	**10%**	**12%**	**13%**	**15%**	**18%**
Purchase trip wire	1	1	2	2	3
Conversion %	**10%**	**7.7%**	**14%**	**11.8%**	**14%**

Tip - Always split test every part of your website.

As you can see from the chart above we managed to increase the number of people visiting the web page over this 21-day period, but half way through, the purchase conversion rate dropped. This chart indentified that we needed to focus on the conversion to get it to the same levels we had at the highest point.

You will also notice that the CTA button was changed twice because the matrix showed us that going to a green button increased our forms being filled in and going to orange did not make much difference. The increase of picture size did get the sales conversion back the percentage we expected. From this you can see what the trip wire conversion rate should be and while you increase the traffic to the page you can ensure that the conversion rates stay the same. In this example getting more traffic to the page meant that that extra audience needed some extra convincing to fill in the form on the page.

This is a simple example to demonstrate how testing and measuring using split-testing will have a profound impact on your website marketing. It moved from 10% trip wire purchase to 14% which is nearly a 50% increase in 21 days. Apply this methodology to all areas of your marketing and you will be laughing.

"Sounds good" said Luke. "I am not too comfortable with numbers but I can see what you are saying here in your example. It will bring everything I have done so far together, and I will be able to analyse what is working and what isn't."

"Great", replied Jack, "I am glad I am helping. We only have one week left and you will know all 7 steps."

7.1 Why follow-up?

"Right Luke", now you have had all the information to add to your website, you now need to learn what to do with the leads you get.

Like any marketing, if you spend a lot of time and effort getting a lead you need to follow it up. This is no different for websites and with it being online you can use many tools to do this automatically.

Throughout the previous weeks we have talked about setting up your website correctly, becoming an expert in getting the right traffic and putting in place things on your website that encourages people to fill in a form to get something in return. If you leave it there you might as well not have bothered.

Now we need to create a follow-up sequence that relates to the original entry point on your website that moves them down the funnel into becoming a customer. In marketing circles there is a guide that says, you need to have nine or more contact points with someone before they feel comfortable buying from you.

This means that from the first point they come into contact with you, they are checking you out to see if they like you and you are building trust. Most people assume that you know how to do or create what you do and they are looking to get to know, like and trust you.

By knowing this as well as your avatar, you can create a basic follow-up process that really resonates with the person who entered your funnel. Even if they don't buy from you after the nine contacts, you should have in place a follow-up process that keeps contacting them with relevant things forever. I often get people who I have previously met many years ago come back to me to buy even though I personally have not met them in that time. Even better, they are much easier to convert because they have built a long-term "like and trust" relationship, where they know me fairly well because of the things I have sent them during that time.

I am sure it goes without saying, but you also need to allow people the chance to not hear from you if they ask not to. Don't get too upset because this shows that your filtering is working. This also works for you too.

For a six-month period I have done several quotes and given lots of advice to a potential prospect only to find that he went to a competitor several times. Each time he complained about the poor service he got from the competitor but kept coming back to me for advice and quotes. I thought that we would win him over but had to take a reality pill and decided to reverse my marketing process by filtering him out myself. He has had more than his fair share of contacts with me to know and like me, but he never came onboard. Now that I have taken him off my list I have much more free time to give to the people who really appreciate my time. He will go onto my continuous follow-up list and can come back if he wants.

To set up a follow up process from a website you need to write a few emails that relate to the download and send them on day 1, 3, 5, 8, 14, 21, 28 and then monthly. This is only a guide to test, as you will know your marketing much better at this stage. As covered in the previous chapter about split-testing and measuring you need to apply that here. At the end of 28 days I would send an email every fortnight for a few months and then move to monthly emails. Once you have mastered this and have a suitable system in place I would suggest sprinkling in a direct mail posting piece and some phone calls. This is a bit more advanced marketing that we will cover in another book in the series.

7.2 How to automate

When you're in business you go through those times when you feel like you're drowning in tasks. I've been there and I expect you've been there too.

When you automate your business by setting up systems, it almost runs itself. It can take time to fit into the pattern but after a while everything you do becomes automatic.

The first thing to do is to sit down and create a plan. Daily, weekly, bi-weekly, monthly, whatever. There are things you need to keep on top of each day, like dealing with emails or running social media. Schedule that in first. Then look at the things you need to do once a week and schedule those in. Then start planning in longer term things.

The key is to schedule things as though you had staff, even if you don't. Make procedures for everything and follow them through. What happens after a customer makes an enquiry? How do you handle a complaint? By having all these things set in stone as though they were the role of individual team members, you can keep things running smoothly even if you're doing it all yourself.

Take a specific look at the areas you struggle with most. The kind of things you keep putting off, but they still hang over you. You know they need doing but they're just not your favourite part of running a business. How can these tasks be made easier? It may be that you need to take a few minutes with a coffee beforehand and then jump straight into them at 9am and not look up from the computer until it's done. Or that Friday is a good way to do it because you've got the weekend to look forward to and you can start fresh on Monday without thinking about it.

The thing is, once all these things are in place and you've been doing them for a while, they become second nature, and you feel calmer and more on top of things.

There are lots of technical solutions to help with automating your business. A CRM (Customer Relationship Management) system is the ultimate one, but there are other solutions available too. Look at email auto-responders. These can be used for all sorts of things, from sending out regular newsletters to keep customers interested, to reminding a customer about an appointment and limiting the risk of missed appointments. You take the initial step of creating the emails and scheduling them, and then forget about them, they go out on their own!

Another place where scheduling comes in really useful is in social media. Look at a tool called *Hootsuite*. This allows you to schedule posts on Facebook, Twitter and LinkedIn to post automatically throughout the day. So you can plan your social media in the morning, and then turn it off and check back later to answer comments and replies. This also saves you from getting distracted by your feeds when you're supposed to be getting on with something else!

If you have a blog, these can be scheduled too, depending on your website platform. So if you have a quiet day, you can use the opportunity for a blogging session and schedule them to go out throughout the week. Keep notes of any good ideas you have and save them for your blogging day. This could even be a weekend or evening if writing is something you enjoy and doesn't feel like a chore.

Another important thing to remember is that multitasking doesn't really work. If you're doing two things at once you can only give them half the attention. If you're doing three things at once, you end up giving each thing even less attention. Schedule a time slot of each job and get on with that job before moving onto the next one. Don't deliberately let your brain get scrambled. Remember the quality of the work you do is more important than the quantity – longer hours doesn't necessarily equal better productivity!

Put the basics in place for your website marketing and once you have a regular amount of leads that convert to customers and you know your conversion numbers you might want to move to the next stage in your business of systemising which we will cover in another book in the series.

Luke says "Thanks for your presentation over the last few weeks. I could not believe that these simple changes would have such a dramatic impact on my business lead generation. Now that we are measuring the results I can see where we need to fix parts of the funnel. I am worried that you are giving too much away in your presentation, what are you trying to sell?"

"Nothing", says Jack. "I want to help others avoid the pain I have gone through over the years and if this is of interest to businesses I might write a book. Let me summarise the 7 steps."

Conclusion

Following these 7 steps, will set your website up right from the beginning. Even if you get other people to create your website, do your graphics or write your copy you will be informed of what you need to make a successful website.

If you are one of those people who turns to the back of a book looking for the one magic answer I am afraid that you need to start at the section on purpose. I can't emphasis enough that you can't start by looking for a beautiful website without having a clear purpose. It builds the foundation not only for your website but all of your marketing.

It does involve a bit of work before you get to do the sexy stuff and seeing it on the Internet, but you need to create your website with a funnel based around what you have learnt about your customer avatar. In the same way that your potential customer will want to get to know you, you need to get to know your potential customer that you are looking for very well first.

Only at this point can you create a useful website that your avatar customer is looking for and the layout will be easy. Your layout will give them just what they are looking for and look the way they expect. You can get them to engage with you by sharing their personal contact details because you have offered them just what they are looking for.

Your website copy will have the words that these prospects use and are searched for on the internet, so you will rank higher because the search engines can see that your visitors like what you offer. Your social media talks the language of your avatar and in the places that they hang out.

Once they are on your website they feel comfortable to be squeezed a little, to share their contact details where you gently follow-up. At each stage you are filtering people out that don't meet your requirements, or are not ready to buy now. You will know the predictable conversion numbers because you test and measure.

Now you have the right people you can follow-up until you build a relationship with them. This is not rocket science and the best way to look at it is if you wanted to find a partner. You go through these stages to build a relationship to get to know them before you might get married.

About the author

Darren Hickie

From a very early age Darren knew he wanted to run a business. His grandmother kept asking him what he wanted to do as a job and when she heard "I want to run a business" she exclaimed "in what". Darren's reply was "I don't know but I think that it does not matter as long as I learn how businesses are run, they should all be similar".

Darren started testing and learning different skills, like buying, repackaging and selling sweets. He also found himself in a huge house on his own with no way to pay the bills and did what came natural to him, rented out rooms.

Setting out by first getting his qualifications in accounting, and then being drawn into IT, where he saw the potential benefits of how this would eventually change the way we work. At that time most people were scared of it and found it difficult to understand, Darren found that he had a natural gift for it.

Having a chance opportunity of sharing his IT skills by teaching at a local school, they also sent him to gain his Adult Education Teaching Certificate.

With this new found confidence of being able to analyse and present while understanding IT, he found a life changing job as a business analyst for a Blue Chip company. He developed his skills and knowledge of how businesses run, and was instrumental in fixing problems and generating new streams of income. He learnt how to manage large teams of people, often with worldwide sub-sections, to deliver projects with million pound+ budgets that generated 10's of millions over the following years.

At this point Darren felt that he had gathered enough skills and experience to go it alone. He worked as a consultant for a London based Blue Chip Company while setting up his own business, delivering IT solutions to small companies.

The first few years of running his company, called *Develop and Promote*, was initially taking what he knew from the corporate world into helping local small business. Along the way he has set-up and sold a few businesses as opportunities came along.

He believes in lifelong learning and that everyone should be able to use IT to their benefit.

This book is part of a series of books to help business owners demystify all the different areas of running a business.

At the time of print these are the planned books and if you have a suggestion for an area I have missed please contact me.

Pricing
Marketing
Finance
You and your people
Property investing
Systemising your business
Sales
Getting the most out of your IT

Further Links

For more information about this series of books and extra information head over to:

www.getsmartaround.com/webbook

You can also register for more details about upcoming books and training in this series.

On the website you will find examples of website marketing that has worked well, cheat sheets and free video training.

I welcome your feedback and open discussion. Together we will create a community to help each other from our experiences. Let share and grow our knowledge.

You can register for free information to accompany this book to enhance your learning here:

www.GetSmartAround.com/WebBook

www.ingramcontent.com/pod-product-compliance
Lightning Source LLC
Chambersburg PA
CBHW051501050726
47593CB00005B/2170